T0156404

Rape...
Survivor Not Victim

Tashia Marie

Order this book online at www.trafford.com
or email orders@trafford.com

Most Trafford titles are also available at major online book retailers.

Note for Librarians: A cataloguing record for this book is available from Library
and Archives Canada at www.collectionscanada.ca/amicus/index-e.html

Printed in Victoria, BC, Canada.

ISBN: 978-1-4269-1644-1 (sc)

*Our mission is to efficiently provide the world's finest, most
comprehensive book publishing service, enabling every author to
experience success. To find out how to publish your book, your way, and
have it available worldwide, visit us online at www.trafford.com*

Trafford rev. 9/8/2009

 www.trafford.com

North America & international
toll-free: 1 888 232 4444 (USA & Canada)
phone: 250 383 6864 ♦ fax: 812 355 4082

Victim. Nothing could be further from the truth. If you have been raped and are alive to read this book then you, my friend, are a survivor. Only the strong survive. I am a firm believer in that what does not kill you will indeed make you stronger.

This book is not a tale of woe and sorrow, it is a celebration of life and the lessons, all be they sometimes harsh, we are here to learn.

When life smacks you across the face,
wake up,
it's trying to get your attention!

Contents

Acknowledgements

I would like to dedicate this book to the people in my life that gave me the unconditional love and strength to survive my tragedy. Together with my family and friends I was able to see past the horror of my situation and into the light of truth of who I am and why this happened.

Mom. You are the inspiration that makes me me. I thank you for your strength and energy. If not for you I may very well have been smothered by the dark veil of depression that lay across my mind. You are the most compassionate and helpful person I have ever known and I am proud to call you mom. I love you.

Dad. Your self-control and calm listening abilities allowed me to vent my anger in safety. Thank you for not judging me. Thank you for never telling me what to do. You allowed me to work things out myself, although I am sure you bit your tongue more than once. I love you.

Brooke and Austin. You are my babies. You are the reason I kept on living. If it were not for the two of you

I would not have had the motivation to keep on going. Knowing that I had to be strong and act in your best interest is why I handled myself honorably in a situation that could have gone so terribly wrong. You are my angels, I will always love and respect you for you. I am blessed to call you my children.

Brett. My wonderful husband. Where do I start? You were the turning point in my life. When I was walking the thin line between being an angry bitterly scorned woman and the real me - happy-go-lucky, positive, loving lady - you gently nudged me towards myself. Words could never express the level of appreciation and love I hold for you. I respect you more than I thought I could ever respect a man. You are the perfect example of what it means to be a man, a husband, a father, a friend, a lover and most of all a human being. Thank you for being you!!!

Me. I do have to thank myself for stopping and accepting all of the above-mentioned people into my life when it could have been so easy to shut them all out. I am also thankful for being able to see the good behind everything that appears evil, the blessing disguised as tragedy. I love the person I have grown to be, it took seven years to get back what I lost, myself. I am stronger and smarter than I was before. If I could go back in time and erase what happened to me on October 2nd, 1999 I can honestly say that I would not. It was only through the pain and anger that I freed my children and myself. I love me.

INTRODUCTION

Have you ever heard the expression, "You have to go through hell to get to heaven?" Well I have and I did. This is my story, my journey of deceit, betrayal, pain, anger and finally closure and true love and happiness.

Only once you have lost everything can you finally truly appreciate what you are and what really matters in this game called life. This is no dress rehearsal - you only have one shot at life.

You are the only person responsible for your level of health, happiness and success. Perception is reality - make it what you want it t be or deal with what you have settled for.

I have learned a lifetime's worth of lessons in the past seven years and I am going to share them with you. Please use what you can, ignore what you wish but always remember, when push comes to shove you are all you have to call your own in this world so you better appreciate, love and respect yourself… even when those closest to you do not.

LIVING THE DISILLUSION

Here I am, 24 years old and a mother of a three-year-old little girl and a one-year-old little boy. I have a common-law husband, we will call him Joe, of four and one-half years. We are living in a brand new home we designed and built in an upscale neighborhood. We are both self-employed and quite successful. You can say I am living the dream - the perfect family, the perfect life. This is when the disillusion begins to fade.

We have problems, like every couple does. Lacks of communication, our interests are varied and of course lack of balance when it comes to dividing up our time between home, family, work and play. The typical family stuff we all go through at one time or another.

It is the morning of October 3rd when I awake to my son's cries. He must be hungry. As I slowly rise out of bed I notice that I am only half dressed. My pants are missing but I am still wearing my sweatshirt from yesterday. As I struggle to get to the kitchen I cannot understand why I am so groggy and unbalanced. I know I have been working a little hard lately but am I really having a nervous breakdown? Is this what it feels like when your brain just shuts off? Maybe I am getting the flu?

As I approach the kitchen I see my son waddling down the hall - he had just learned to walk about a month earlier. My mouth is dry and pasty, I can barely kiss him let alone say good morning. I swerve left towards the stove to turn it on so I can make some pancakes for breakfast.

As I turn around to retrieve the batter from the pantry I notice my son is picking something up off the floor. In front of the television are the pillows and blankets Joe and I were laying on the night before when we had watched some movies we rented. Come to think of it, how did that movie end?

Suddenly I realize my son is about to put the object he found on the floor into his mouth. Quickly grabbing it out of his hand I am shocked to see the object is a red and yellow pill capsule. This is not mine, how did it get here? What is it?

Just then Joe appears from around the corner, entering the front room. "Is this yours?" I ask him. A look of shock suddenly washes over his face.

Silence…

"What is this?" I ask Joe again.

"Nothing." he mumbles while moving towards the kitchen. "It's nothing."

"Nothing? What do you mean? How can -"

"It's nothing!" he interrupts.

"No!" I reply. "What is this? Our son almost ate it."

I am so dizzy, I can't stand anymore. I turn towards the kitchen counter, pulling myself up on top of it so I can sit and rest.

"It's for my sinuses." Joe finally responds.

"What the hell is it doing on the floor in the front room?" I snap back instantly, I can feel his fear. Something is wrong here.

"Oh, it must have fallen out of my pocket last night, c'mon, want me to make breakfast?" Joe offers.

Now my alarm bells are going off, Joe never offers to do anything for me, ever. Something is very wrong. That look on his face, he's scared, but why?

Next to me I notice the empty ice cream bowls from last night. Yes, that's right ... We were watching the movie, Joe got up to get some ice cream and brought me some as well.

"You don't have sinus problems." I bark.

"Um, well, they help me sleep too." Joe quickly adds.

"Sleeping pill?" I murmur. Wait a minute, I remember a show that was on television the other week. Something about a guy at a bar who drugs women with a sedative in their drink and then rapes them in his van. The drug caused a mild form of amnesia so the women wouldn't remember what had happened to them or who had done it.

The ice cream bowls… "You drugged me! In the ice cream!"

"No, no I broke the capsule in my ice cream to clear my sinuses." Joe insists.

"But you just said these help you to sleep. Besides, you always swallow your Tylenol and then take a drink of water. You're not a baby, you don't crush pills in your ice cream - you drugged me, why are my pants on the floor? How did I get to bed? What have you done?" I scream at him. Now I am crying and starting to shake. I think I am going to throw up.

Joe comes closer and hugs me tight. "I didn't do anything wrong. I never did anything wrong." A dark heavy cloud of confusion envelopes me, his words seem surreal.

"What?" I sob.

"Maybe I gave you the wrong bowl by mistake." Joe whispers.

I pull back, almost falling off the counter. "What is this pill?" I scream. I can feel the adrenaline starting to course through my body. I am starting to sweat as the anger swells inside me.

"I told you it's for my sinuses." Joe insists.

"No! What is it called?!!" I yell.

"It's Sinutab." Joe snaps at me as he takes a step back.

I examine the red and blue pill, inscribed on the side is APO 30. "No! Sinutab says Sinutab on the side not APO 30! What is this? What have you done?" I plead.

"I didn't do anything wrong!" Joe insists.

"Fine if you won't tell me I'll find out myself." Jumping off the counter I stagger towards the bedroom. While quickly dressing I notice I am bleeding lightly from between my legs. As I head towards the front door I stop and give Joe one last opportunity to tell me the truth. "Last chance, what is this?"

"I told you already, stop freaking out and acting all crazy. You always blow things out of proportion like this." Joe remarks, trying to belittle me and place a seed of doubt in my mind.

"I'll be back. Stay here and feed the kids breakfast." is all I can muster up. I feel like I am floating in a fog of dense almost suffocating numbness. I can't think nothing makes sense. Is this a dream? Am I even awake? This can't be real, can it? "I'll be right back." I hear myself babble as I slam the door behind me.

REALITY HITS HARD

"Do you want to press charges?" questions the constable from across the desk.

"What?" I mumble, still groggy and confused.

"If you do not wish to press charges," replies the constable, "we are prepared to go ahead any way."

"I just came down here to find out what this pill is, the drug store is not open until 11:00am." I explain.

"You have been drugged with a prescription sedative and probably sexually assaulted." The constable informs me.

"Raped? Oh no, that couldn't happen. I mean we are basically married, we have two children." I try to reason with him.

"We have called in a female officer to escort you to the hospital. She will accompany you through the procedure." The officer advises me.

"Procedure, hospital, what do you mean?" I hear myself asking from some far off place. My mind is racing in a messy muddy circle. What do I do? Where do I go? Are they talking to me?

"This is serious," insists the officer. "You are in shock and need medical attention."

"I need a cigarette. Do you smoke?" I have no clue as to what is going on here.

"No, but I will find one for you. I'll be right back." the officer assures me.

The trip to the hospital seems like a movie or a play, not real in any way. I seem to have no sense of understanding of what is happening, it feels like a daydream – almost real but not quite. I never figured it would be so quiet riding in a cop car, smooth and silent. I think this is what death might sound like. I hope we don't stop. We can just keep driving right?

All I wanted was an answer about some stupid little pill. Now it's been two and one-half hours of being questioned by 3 or 4 or 5 different RCMP detectives about the night before. Now here I am with a female officer and 2 nurses being poked and prodded by some emergency room doctor. He looks up from between my legs to coldly inform me that I have a lateral tear in my cervix and semen residue inside me. The voices fade softly to a whisper as the fluorescent ceiling lights flood the room and wash everything away. I feel sick, I'm going to throw up this time for sure.

"Are you ok?" I hear one of the nurses asking me as she tries to get me to sit up on the examination bed.

Now I lose it. How can this be real? Me. Drugged and raped. By my own husband and father of my two children.

"Your blood work came back positive for a

Temazepam, it's a prescription sedative. What do you remember?" Questions the doctor.

Again, for the fifth time or is this the sixth time? Doesn't really matter I guess. So I begin to tell them what I can recall, which is basically nothing between the hours of 8:45pm and 5:30am of the previous evening.

They are taking my pants as evidence so I have to leave the hospital in those ugly teal cotton pants. Heading back to the police station I still don't know for sure if this is just a bad dream or what. Maybe some sick joke or something, it has to be.

"We are going to arrest him now." states the officer.

"My kids. They are at home with him, I need to get them first." I beg.

"OK. We will be right behind you." The officer assures me.

As I pull into the driveway I notice Joe's truck is gone. They're gone! All three of them are gone! I think the phone is ringing, or is this just wishful thinking? No, this is cold and calculating, it's Joe.

"Hello?" my voice squeaks out.

"I'm not coming home just to be arrested." Joe's voice bluntly warns.

"What are you talking about?" I snarl trying to sound irritated so he won't guess the police are here. "Get home, I didn't give you the car seats, you can't be driving with the kids in that truck without their seats! Jesus Joe, you don't even have a license, what if you get stopped?" I scold.

"OK, but I need to explain what happened, maybe I mixed up the bowls by accident and you got mine." He bargains in his usual manipulative way.

"OK, drive careful!" I hang up the phone before my voice starts to quiver from my fear. Oh my God, Joe has his grandfather's rifle in the truck.

Looking into the kitchen sink I see one large ceramic soup bowl and one little plastic kids bowl. There is no way in hell he could have mixed the bowls up! This is not a dream! This is real!

I see Joe pull up the road and he notices the ghost car across from our driveway. He drives past our house to the end of the cul-de-sac. Oh my God, he's going to make a run for it! I run onto the road screaming and waving my arms frantically! The neighbors are looking at me in my hospital pants as the black F350 is coming at me. Thankfully Joe stops and turns into the driveway.

Joe steps out of the truck and asks me to take the kids inside so they don't have to see him being arrested. He is arrested and charged with administering a noxious substance to overcome resistance & sexual assault causing bodily harm.

After getting the kids ready for bed I call my best friend, "Joe drugged and raped me, get over here and bring smokes."

The very next day the kids and I move to another city to live with my mother. 18 long and eventful months later Joe pleads guilty and gets time served, a slap on the wrist this time…

FIRST THINGS FIRST

The two most important words you will ever hear ... Restraining Order. Don't even think twice about it - do it, immediately.

The RCMP automatically placed a restraining order against Joe for my protection. I know for a fact that if it had not been for this single step I would have gone back to Joe. I would probably be dead by now, not to mention what may have happened to my children.

Joe, like most manipulators, would have been able to convince me that it was not his fault, he was sorry or maybe that I wanted it. It is sad I know, but it would have probably happened. You see I was willing to sacrifice my happiness, my dreams and my life for the chance for my children to have their father. Is that not the main reason why women stay in unhealthy and abusive relationships, for the kids?

This is the biggest lie we tell ourselves. Think about it, if you were a kid, which would you choose? Having mom and dad living together and constantly arguing and yelling, never touching or kissing? Surrounded by tension, seeing mom unhappy all the time, learning this is what a normal family unit is? Or, mom loving and hugging you? Sure she may have to work part time or even full time but there is no anger, no yelling, there is only togetherness. The lessons you learn from her are to be strong, to make it on your own and most of all to love yourself enough to be safe and happy. I, personally, would pick the second scenario - and I did. The role model you are to yourself is the same role model you are to your kids.

Do not ever say anything bad about what has happened. Don't lie, but don't hurt your kids with your words or descriptions of what happened. If it was a friend, family member or husband, a little white lie is better than traumatizing a young mind.

I blamed our moving away and not seeing dad on Joe's job. "Daddy's boss made him work far away and he misses you and he loves you very much." I would say. This, of course, is an age sensitive issue - just use compassion and common sense. Put the love and sense of security for your babies ahead of your intense anger and pain, you are the adult here.

Stay Focused

I found that throwing myself into my work provided me with an avenue to expel my energies. Of course there were many occasions where I screamed, yelled and broke things, but I did that in private. You must take time or make time to cry. Crying cleanses your soul. It dilutes your anger and lets you feel the pain and betrayal.

If you can feel the hurt you can start to heal the hurt.

You must first remove the poison before you can clean and tend to your wounds. If you do not remove the poison of the attack, your emotional wounds will become infected and fester, creating a huge swollen soar on your soul.

Keep Living

Do not let him win by letting him take your life away from you. Remember, you are still the same person you were before the rape and maybe even a little better. You survived. You are wiser and stronger than you were before the attack.

Do the things you used to do. I like to dance, so I danced everyday and it helped me feel alive. Don't take me wrong, I still had a huge chip on my shoulder and hated men, but I still had to get up each morning and face another day. After all, it is Joe who is sick not me.

It's Him, Not You, That's Broken

I don't care who says sometimes rape is provoked, they are full of ignorance and denial. Nobody has the right to force anybody into doing anything. Only a weak and pathetic individual is consumed by the need to overpower another human being, especially someone who is physically weaker.

When you consider my case and cases like it, I think it is safe to double the pathetic level. I mean really, he had to drug me into unconsciousness! Even after the fact that there was unlimited trust built into the relationship. That's sad and sick!

THE SIX STEPS OF HEALING

Everyone has heard about or read about the six stages of healing. I am not going to explain each one here as they are self-evident in their names.

1. Denial
2. Self-blame
3. Victim
4. Indignation (anger)
5. Survival
6. Integration (acceptance)

All I want to impart here is the fact that we do indeed have to go through and genuinely complete each and every one of these steps IN ORDER. There is no skipping any one stage or you are just lying to yourself. If you do skip a step you will complete the remaining stages only to fall back into the trap of the stage you were too afraid to complete the first time.

I learned this first hand in my sexual assault group

therapy class. I witnessed women skip a stage and go on to almost complete the program only to completely fall apart at the end and go right back to stage one. It's hard and it hurts but you have to do it to learn and grow and heal.

Having had such a loss of control during the rape it only makes sense to me that you would not want to lose control again in one or more of the stages of healing. For example, you are not losing control if you cry your eyes out for days or weeks in the victim stage. This is a cleansing of your soul. Your tears will wash away the darkness and grime from the recesses of your mind so you can stop being scared and start being alive again.

These steps are painful but necessary and I wish you the best.

Be honest with yourself....

Warning Signs of Unhealthy Relationships and the Self-Defeating Games we Play

Personally, I am very familiar with each and every one of the self-defeating games. I am also very proud to acknowledge that after years of conscious work I am no longer a victim of my own games and choose each day not to partake in their destructive course. I am free, and so can you be...

The first four games have a common thread between them, they are the tell tale signs that we do not know who we are. We play these games when we believe we may be somewhere between who we think are and who we wish we could be.

The next three games are prevalent in our lives when we cannot determine what is real and what is the distorted illusions resulting from our fears. Fear is, after all, false evidence appearing real.

The following four games are hurdles we encounter when we are struggling to gain personal power. We feel the need for recognition but all too often we settle for attention, be it positive or negative.

Finally, the final two games are the most destructive of all games. We fall victim to these games when we feel and believe that we do not have the power to control our own lives. It is because of this feeling of helplessness we either escape life by altering our reality and thusly our perceptions of it or focus on dominating others and controlling their lives.

I'm Not Good Enough

This is the basic foundation for all self-defeating games. To actually believe we are not good enough fertilizes our minds, preparing them for the seeds of evil thoughts and destructive behavior. If we are not good enough, in whatever aspect of our lives, then we will consciously or unconsciously see our faults in others and project our self-hatred towards them.

People around us are our mirrors. Usually, when we see weaknesses or faults in others and it sparks a strong negative emotion in us, stop and think. That person is reflecting that exact aspect of ourselves, which we dislike, that is why we have such a strong emotion attached to it. If something makes you defensive, there may be a grain of truth to it.

To believe we are not good enough allows ourselves to become lazy and to not even bother trying. Why should we? We are just a victim of circumstances, right? This clouded belief system takes away any accountability on our part and places blame for our situations on society, our families, our backgrounds, our education or whatever else is readily available to make the scapegoat.

We are the only one who could believe this lie. Nobody else can ever claim that we are not good enough, only we know the truth, we are the truth, let's claim our ability - try. If we fail at least we gave it our best shot. With every failure comes knowledge of either how to do it better or how not to do it again, either way we have learned something about ourselves - we are strong enough to face a fear or a challenge. The only failure in life is failing to try.

Gossip

This may seem like a trivial pass time and maybe even a casual icebreaker but let me assure you that this is the first, worst and hardest habit to defeat. Gossip is the way in which the insecure vent their self-anger onto others. When we gossip about another we are only trying to make ourselves feel better. Maybe even feel better than them. To attain a healthy level of self-esteem we need not attack the faults in others. Rather, we should learn from their mistakes and misfortunes and not mock or revel in their pain.

Someone once told me it is a great talent to learn from the mistakes of others. After all, we cannot possibly live long enough to make all the mistakes ourselves. These mistakes are necessary to learn what it is to become truly self-aware and self-evident.

I Am Right

Wow! This was my biggest hurdle on the path to self-discovery. When we feel the need to be right and we know we are right but there is no convincing the other person, the course we take against them may be aggressive or passive depending on the level of security of that relationship.

If the relationship is strong we may act hostile and defensive, actively causing fights and arguments. If the relationship is casual we may take a more passive approach, twisting the facts to make them wrong leaving us as the misunderstood innocent victim.

If we truly are right does it really matter if the other person believes it? We need to ask ourselves these two questions, "Would I rather be right or be happy? In a hundred years will this matter?" In life, our reality, our world is based on our perception of it. Thusly if we are right, then it is so, it does not matter what the other person believes.

Be careful when this game appears, are we trying to prove our point of view or are we just trying to defeat the other person in a power struggle. If we are trying to win to gain power of control over a person or a situation then we have just sabotaged ourselves. If we were truly right, then we would remain content in the surety of that fact and not waste our time and energy arguing against a falsity. Truth always prevails.

Get Them Before They Get Me

This is a pitiful example of erroneous behavior. If we hurt someone else and defend our actions by claiming they would have done it to us, we just beat them to it, then we need to grow up. Never do anything in reaction to an event which has not even happened yet. Stop living in the future! The future is not set so this whole defense is a lie. Live in the present. We would not be able to drive a car accurately while staring in the rearview mirror or looking a hundred yards ahead. If we live honestly with ourselves in the present then we need not worry about negative possibilities, only positive actualities.

We cannot change the past nor can we predict the future. All we can do is live exquisitely in the present, one day at a time. Be real, be ourselves. Do not try to anticipate another person's thoughts or actions and then blame that fantasy for your actions or words.

The fear that someone is at sometime going to do something that will harm us is only securing that which we fear. The things we focus on and think about in life are what we will manifest for ourselves. If our words and our reality are our own perception and analysis of external stimulus, then we had better make certain our minds, our windows to the world, are clean and clear. We cannot see nor understand clearly while we are looking through a streaked and clouded pane.

Don't Participate - Quit

This is admitting failure without even trying. Life is not a dress rehearsal this is the big show. We usually only get one shot at any given situation in life, we cannot rewind the tape. Fear of failure is the biggest downfall of personal growth. If we are trying then we are not failing for true failure comes only from never daring to begin.

Again, remember, fear is only false evidence appearing real. The path to becoming a winner is to never let the illusions created by fear control our lives.

TELL LIES

To tell lies is to erode the very foundation of who we are. If we find ourselves telling lies the only person we are really hurting is ourselves. Most people despise liars, so we in fact are creating a self-hatred, which only compounds with each lie. The scary thing about lies is that if we tell them long enough we will begin to believe them. This can seriously blur our perception of reality.

Keeping our mind clean and clear is fundamental. Lies are like dust, they collect in the corners of your mind, they litter the floor of your conscience and over enough time they can blanket every aspect of your thoughts. Given enough time, lies can and will spread out into all areas of your life, your thoughts, your words and your actions.

HIDE BEHIND JUDGMENTS

To judge another person is to place a false label on a complex, ever changing, and ever evolving person. There is no way we can know what has happened to a person in their past or even their present which makes them act or live the way they do. To pass judgment on someone or to presume to know what would be best for them means you are speaking from a self-appointed place of righteousness. People are who they are and are where they are at any time in their life because of choices they did or did not make. To judge someone on any one point is to be ignorant to every other aspect of his or her being. Don't do it. Do not judge - accept. Accept people for who they are and where they are in their life's journey.

Now let me be very clear here... acceptance is not forgiveness or love. Acceptance is the release of any negative emotions toward another person and just knowing they are who they are at this particular moment in time. To accept someone as they are allows us to retain control over our emotions and thoughts and to remain peaceful. We have no right to change people or their behaviors. If we disagree with their beliefs or become harmed by their actions we must keep our distance, hereby accepting responsibility for our own peace.

ACT ANGRY, START A FIGHT

To allow ourselves to become angry is to release control of ourselves over to the other person. This usually happens when we feel the other person has all the power or control in the relationship. Nobody can make us feel anything, we allow ourselves to get caught up in his or her emotional energy. We are in control of our actions, or at least we should be! Anger only allows the other person to accept a feeling of empowerment. If they have the power to make us mad then they win, we have just given them our power. When we allow ourselves to become angry we do stupid things, we know we have. How many times, if we could, would we take back words or actions born from anger? Anger is like blinders, allowing us to only see our point of view and blocking out any chance of intelligent communication. We should never try to solve the problem when we are angry. Take a break, take a walk and take time to cool down before going back into the situation, this way the outcome will not carry the baggage of regret.

BE A PROBLEM

Being a problem is usually a cry for attention. If we don't get positive attention then negative will do. This could also be caused by jealousy towards the other person. If we feel the other person is well organized and efficient in their life we may try to sabotage them by being a problem. These are the actions of a spoiled child. Grow up!

HIDE BEHIND CONFUSION

To act like we do not understand something and therefore are ignorant to the outcome is our own fault. If we are unclear we must search for clarity. To pretend we don't get it is a reflection of our laziness. We have to start taking charge of our lives, taking charge of ourselves because this is our life so we better understand it. If we live in the cloud of confusion we will never be able to see where we are going. If we do not have goals in and for our lives how will we know if we are heading in the right direction? You wouldn't take a road trip without a map with a marked route, points of interest, a final destination and a time line would you? Then why would you live your life without one?

Break Agreements

To break an agreement is to let ourselves down. Not only do we disappoint the person with whom we have made the agreement with but we also levee a solid blow to our own self-esteem. If we cannot keep our word to others how can we look ourselves in the mirror and feel good and honorable. We need to keep our agreements, if we cannot keep them, we should not make them. There is less shame is admitting we are unable to do something than to have it snowball over time and weigh daily on our mind.

Controlling or Manipulative

This is the epitome of lack of self-esteem. If we feel the need to control or manipulate others we really need to stop and look at our own lives. There is something we have lost all personal power over and we need to get it back. Maybe it is our finances, our career, our daily routine, our children, our sexuality... Whatever the area may be we need to immediately focus on it. Take back that area of our life, reroute it and stop trying to fill the void of control over ourselves by attempting to control others.

Drugs or Alcohol

This is the ultimate escape from reality. If we need to abuse substances to deal with or escape from dealing with our lives - STOP. Whatever we are running from this will not help. We cannot run away from ourselves - wherever we go there we are. These substances are only a temporary escape from our lives. Our lives will never ever change unless we address our demons. We have to live with ourselves for the rest of our lives so we better like ourselves. If there is something that needs to be said, say it. If there is something that needs to be done, do it. If there is something that needs to be changed, change it.

If we are unable to face these challenges alone we need to ask someone we trust to help us. Everybody needs a shoulder to cry on or a hand to hold for strength at some point in their lives. Nobody has done everything on their own - we were all babies at some point weren't we? Our lives will be no better than the plans we make and the actions we take and we need to be thinking clearly in order to plan.

Knowing is the fist step to correcting. Hopefully the lessons I learned can be helpful for you too. I truly believe that life is way too short to have to learn all of its lessons yourself. If you can, learn as much as you can from other people's mistakes and accomplishments.

And remember, it's never too late to heal, unless you wait until you're dead. What are you waiting for?